DISCOVERING MAPS

Country Maps

Harriet Brundle
and John Willis

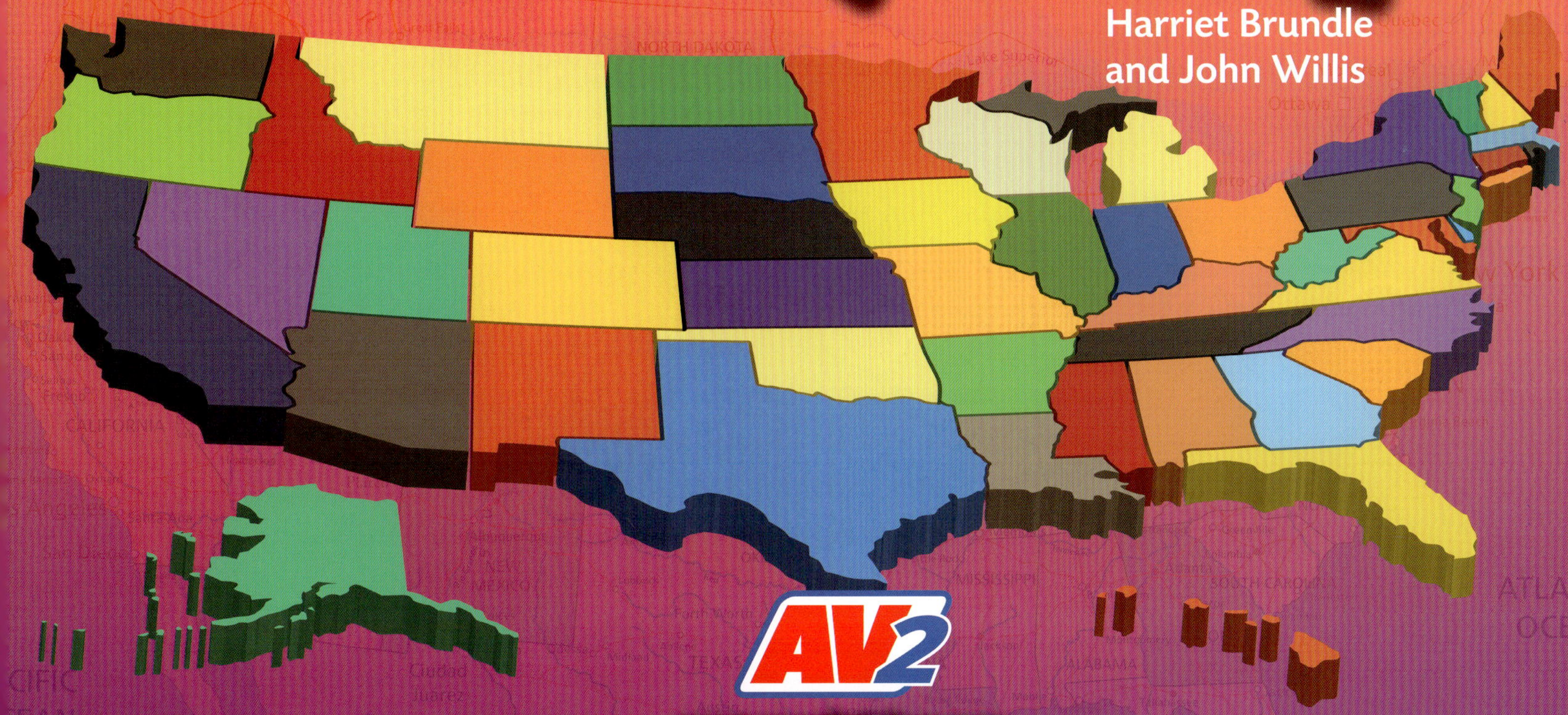

AV2

www.openlightbox.com

ISBN 978-1-7911-3320-7

Country Maps

CONTENTS

What Is a Map?

A map is a picture that gives people information about an **area**. Maps can show many different things, such as **roads**, **population**, or **weather**.

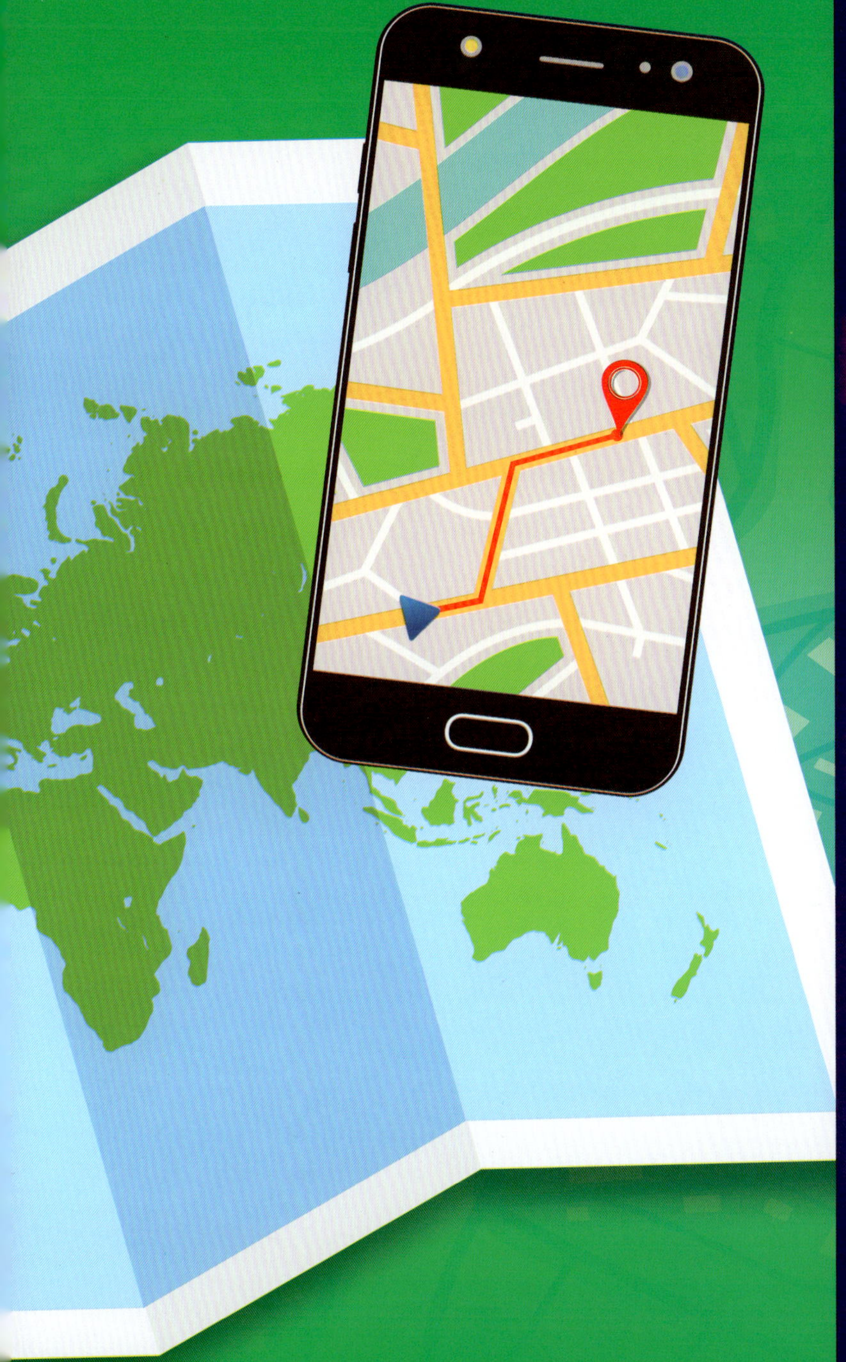

Types of Maps

Political Maps

Show state borders. Often include state capitals along with other cities and towns.

Physical Maps

Show geographical features. Use shading to show how high above sea level land is.

Economic Maps

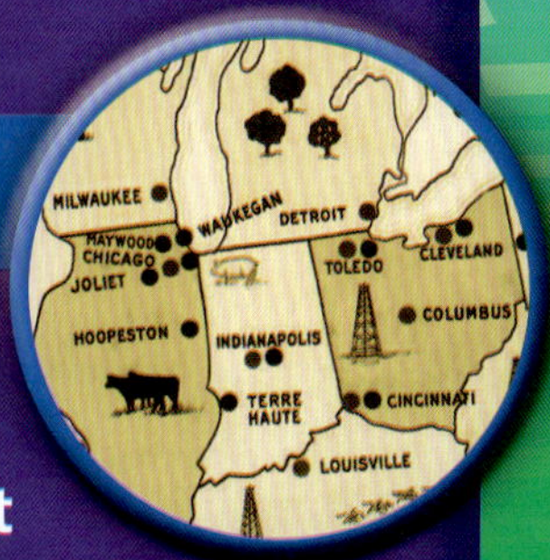

Show the natural resources or major businesses in different parts of a country.

Using a Map

Maps have different colors or symbols. These represent towns, cities, or other landmarks.

Landmarks can include statues or monuments. A mountain or canyon may also be a landmark.

Map Legend

Often, the symbols on a map look like the places they represent. People can also use a key to check what the symbols mean.

Key

Maps are drawn from a "bird's-eye view." This means that they show how the country looks from above.

Each map usually has a compass printed on it. This shows which way on the map is north, south, east, or west.

Scale

Everything on a map has been made smaller, or "scaled down" to fit. The amount by which something is made smaller is called the scale.

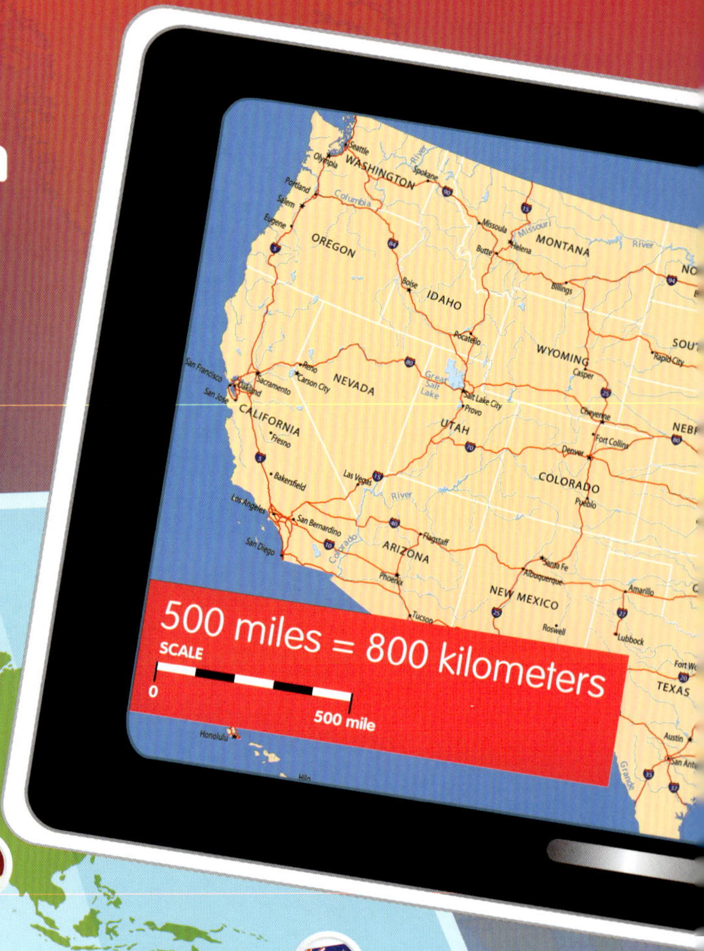

A scale means people can use a map to show **distance**. If people want to know how long a road is, they can use the map scale.

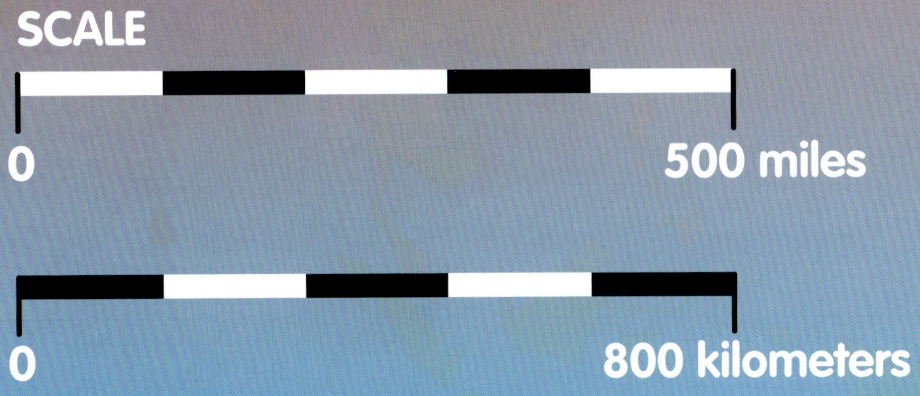

Country Maps

Country maps often show all the different **regions** within that nation.

A map of a country will often show the **landforms**, too.

Country maps might show the different roads and other types of **transportation** across a country instead.

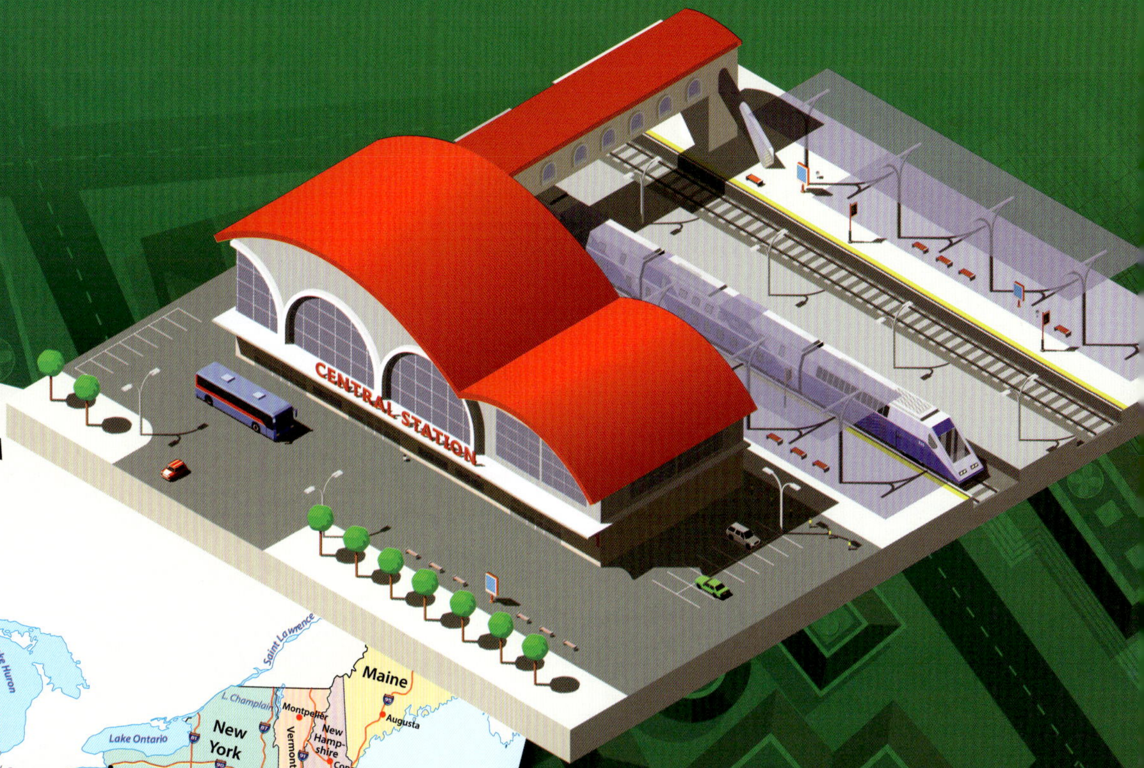

Transportation shown on a map can include train tracks or airports.

Why Use a Country Map?

If you wanted to travel somewhere, you might use a map of that country to help you find your way.

The oldest map showing what is now the United States was made more than 500 years ago.

A map might show where a particular country is in the world and which other countries are nearby.

How Is a Country Map Made?

To make a map of a country, start by drawing the outline of the country. Then, add the country's regions.

Next, any important landmarks can be added. Then, add landforms such as rivers.

Mapping a Country

CHOOSE A COUNTRY

Start by thinking about the country you would like to map.

DRAW THE OUTLINE

Try to draw the outline of the country you chose.

LANDMARKS AND LANDFORMS

Make a list of any of the country's landmarks or landforms that you know.

CREATE A KEY

Create symbols for the points of interest. Then, add them to the map in the correct places.

Be Creative!

This is a map of the U.S. mainland. The borders of each state have been marked with white lines.

Using another map of the United States, can you work out on this map which state is which?

KEY WORDS

Research has shown that as much as 65 percent of all written material published in English is made up of 300 words. These 300 words cannot be taught using pictures or learned by sounding them out. They must be recognized by sight. This book contains 95 common sight words to help young readers improve their reading fluency and comprehension. This book also teaches young readers several important content words, such as proper nouns.

Page	Sight Words First Appearance
4	a, about, an, as, can, different, gives, is, many, or, people, picture, show, such, that, things, what
5	above, along, and, country, high, how, in, land, of, often, other, parts, sea, state, to, use, with
6	also, be, have, may, mountain, these
7	like, look, mean, on, places, river, the, they
8	are, eye, from, this
9	each, has, it, way, which
10	been, by, down, made, miles
11	if, know, long, want
12	all, might, too, will
14	find, help, more, now, than, was, why, years, you, your
15	where, world
16	add, make, start, then
17	any, important, next
18	would
19	try
20	list
21	for, points, them

Page	Content Words First Appearance
4	area, information, map, population, roads, weather
5	borders, businesses, capitals, cities, features, resources, sea level, towns
6	canyon, colors, landmarks, monuments, statues, symbols
7	cafe, key, legend, phone, railway, restaurant
8	view
9	compass
10	amount, kilometers, scale
11	distance
12	landforms, nation, regions, transportation
13	airports, train tracks
14	United States
16	outline

Published by Lightbox Learning Inc.
276 5th Avenue, Suite 704 #917
New York, NY 10001
Website: www.openlightbox.com

Library of Congress Control Number available upon request.

ISBN 978-1-5105-6359-9 (hardcover)
ISBN 979-8-8745-1507-2 (softcover)
ISBN 978-1-5105-6360-5 (static multi-user eBook)
ISBN 978-1-5105-8146-3 (interactive multi-user eBook)

Printed in Guangzhou, China
1 2 3 4 5 6 7 8 9 0 28 27 26 25 24

052024
100923

Project Coordinator: John Willis
Designer: Jean Faye Rodriguez

Every reasonable effort has been made to trace ownership and to obtain permission to reprint copyright material. The publisher would be pleased to have any errors or omissions brought to its attention so that they may be corrected in subsequent printings.

The publisher acknowledges Getty Images and Shutterstock as the primary image suppliers for this title.

First published by BookLife in 2018